Official Rules of Tennis

USTA™

TRIUMPH
BOOKS
CHICAGO

This book is available in quantity at special discounts for your group or organization. For further information, contact:

Triumph Books
601 South LaSalle Street
Chicago, Illinois 60605
(312) 939-3330
Fax (312) 663-3557

Printed in Canada.

ISBN 1-57243-341-8

This cover and design treatment copyright © Triumph Books.
Cover photo by Russ Adams courtesy of the United States Tennis Association.
Typography: Sue Knopf.

User's Guide

This edition of the *Official Rules of Tennis* has been designed to give tennis fans of all ages a quick and easy reference guide to the action on the court.

This edition contains the following material, in the format indicated:

The *Rules of Tennis*, as drafted by the International Tennis Federation, of which the United States Tennis Association (USTA) is a member.

The Code, a player's guide for unofficiated matches, published by the USTA.

USTA Comments
provide the reader with supplementary information intended to help clarify the rules. The United States Tennis Association drafts these comments.

ITF Notes *provide additional information to the section of the rule being referenced. The International Tennis Federation drafts these notes.*

Contents

The
Singles
Game

1. THE COURT

The Court shall be a rectangle 78 feet (23.77m.) long and 27 feet (8.23m.) wide.

USTA Comment
See Rule 34 for a doubles court.

It shall be divided across the middle by a net suspended from a cord or metal cable of a maximum diameter of one-third of an inch (0.8cm.), the ends of which shall be attached to, or pass over, the tops of two posts, which shall be not more than 6 inches (15cm.) square or 6 inches (15cm.) in diameter. These posts shall not be higher than 1 inch (2.5cm.) above the top of the net cord. The centres of the posts shall be 3 feet (.914m.) outside the Court on each side and the height of the posts shall be such that the top of the cord or metal cable shall be 3 feet 6 inches (1.07m.) above the ground.

When a combined doubles (see Rule 34) and singles Court with a doubles net is used for singles, the net must be supported to a height of 3 feet 6 inches (1.07m.) by means of two posts, called "singles sticks," which shall be not more than 3 inches (7.5cm.) square or 3 inches (7.5cm.) in diameter. The centres of the singles sticks shall be 3 feet (.914m.) outside the singles Court on each side.

The net shall be extended fully so that it fills completely the space between the two posts and shall be of sufficiently small mesh to prevent the ball passing through. The height of the net shall be 3 feet (.914m.) at the centre, where it shall be held down taut by a strap not more than 2 inches (5cm.) wide and completely white in colour. There shall be a band covering the cord or metal cable and the top of the net of not less than 2 inches (5cm.) nor more than 2½ inches (6.35cm.) in depth on each side and completely white in colour. There shall be no advertisement on the net, strap, band or singles sticks.

USTA Comment

The following is an approved method for obtaining proper net tautness. First, loosen the center strap. Next, tighten the net cord until it is approximately 40 inches above the ground, being careful not to overtighten the net. Finally, tighten the center strap until the center of the net is 36 inches above the ground. These measurements should always be made before the first match of the day.

The lines bounding the ends and sides of the Court shall respectively be called the base-lines and the side-lines. On each side of the net, at a distance of 21 feet (6.40m.) from it and parallel with it, shall be drawn the service-lines. The space on each side of the net between the service-line and the side-lines shall be divided into two equal parts called the service-courts by the centre service-line, which must be 2 inches (5cm.) in width, drawn half-way between, and parallel with, the side-lines. Each base-line shall be bisected by an imaginary continuation of the centre service-line to a line 4 inches (10cm.) in length and 2 inches (5cm.) in width called the "centre mark" drawn inside the Court, at right angles to and in contact with such base-lines. All other lines shall be not less than 1 inch (2.5cm.) nor more than 2 inches (5cm.)

in width, except the base-line, which may be not more than 4 inches (10cm.) in width, and all measurements shall be made to the outside of the lines. All lines shall be of uniform colour. If advertising or any other material is placed at the back of the Court, it may not contain white or yellow. A light colour may only be used if this does not interfere with the vision of the players.

If advertisements are placed on the chairs of the linesmen sitting at the back of the court, they may not contain white or yellow. A light colour may only be used if this does not interfere with the vision of the players.

> *ITF Note 1: In Davis Cup, Fed Cup and the Official Championships of the International Tennis Federation, specific requirements with regard to the space behind the baseline and at the sides are included in the respective Regulations for these events.*

> *ITF Note 2: At club or recreational level, the space behind each baseline should be not less than 18 feet (5.5m.) and at the sides not less than 10 feet (3.05m.).*

2. PERMANENT FIXTURES

The permanent fixtures of the Court shall include not only the net, posts, singles sticks, cord or metal cable, strap and band, but also, where there are any such, the back and side stops, the stands, fixed or movable seats and chairs round the Court, and their occupants, all other fixtures around and above the Court, and the Umpire, Net-cord Judge, Footfault Judge, Linesmen and Ball Boys when in their respective places.

> **ITF Note:** *For the purpose of this Rule, the word "Umpire" comprehends the Umpire, the persons entitled to a seat on the Court, and all those persons designated to assist the Umpire in the conduct of a match.*

3. THE BALL

Balls that are approved for play under the Rules of Tennis must comply with the following specifications:

a. The ball shall have a uniform outer surface consisting of a fabric cover and shall be white or yellow in colour. If there are any seams they shall be stitchless.

b. The ball shall conform to the requirements specified in Appendix I (Regulations for making tests specified in Rule 3.), Section (iv) for size and be more than 1.975 ounces (56.0 grams) and less than 2.095 ounces (59.4 grams) in weight.

c. The ball shall have a bound of more than 53 inches (134.62cm.) and less than 58 inches (147.32cm.) when dropped 100 inches (254.00cm.) upon a flat, rigid surface, e.g., concrete. The ball shall have a forward deformation of more than .220 of an inch (.559cm.) and less than .290 of an inch (.737cm.) and a return deformation of more than .315 of an inch (.800cm.) and less than .425 of an inch (1.080cm.) at 18 lb. (8.165kg.) load. The two deformation figures shall be the averages of three individual readings along three axes of the ball and no two individual readings shall differ by more than .030 of an inch (.076cm.) in each case.

d.   For play above 4,000 feet (1219m.) in altitude above sea level, two additional types of ball may be used. The first type is identical to those described above except that the bound shall be more than 48 inches (121.92cm.) and less than 53 inches (134.62cm.) and the ball shall have an internal pressure that is greater than the external pressure. This type of tennis ball is commonly known as a pressurized ball. The second type is identical to those described above except that they shall have a bound of more than 53 inches (134.62cm.) and less than 58 inches (147.32cm.) and shall have an internal pressure that is approximately equal to the external pressure and have been acclimatised for 60 days or more at the altitude of the specific tournament. This type of tennis ball is commonly known as a zero-pressure or non-pressurised ball.

e.   All tests for bound, size and deformation shall be made in accordance with the regulations in Appendix I.

f.   The International Tennis Federation shall rule on the question of whether any ball or prototype complies with the above specifications or is otherwise approved for play. Such ruling may be taken on its own initiative, or upon application by any party with a bona fide interest therein, including any player, equipment manufacturer or National Association or members thereof. Such rulings and applications shall be made in accordance with the applicable Review and Hearing Procedures of the International Tennis Federation (see Appendix II).

ITF Note 1: *Any ball to be used in a tournament which is played under the Rules of Tennis must be named on the official ITF list of approved balls issued by the International Tennis Federation.*

ITF Note 2: *From 1st January 2000 until 31st December 2001 two further types of tennis ball may be used on an experimental basis.*

The first type is identical to those described in paragraphs a. to c. above except that the ball shall have a forward deformation of more than .195 inches (.495 cm.) and less than .235 inches (.597 cm.) and return deformation of more than .295 inches (.749 cm.) and less than .380 inches (.965 cm.). This type of ball shall be described as ball type 1 and may be used in either a pressurised or non-pressurised form.

Another type is identical to those described in paragraphs a. to c. above except that the size shall be more than 2.750 inches (6.985 cm.) and less than 2.875 inches (7.302 cm.) in diameter as determined by ring gauges and detailed in Appendix I Section iv. This type of ball shall be described as ball type 3 and may be used in either a pressurised or non-pressurised form.

All other types of ball defined by Rule 3 shall be described as ball type 2.

For the purpose of tournaments played under this experiment:

1. *Ball type 1 (fast) should only be used for play on court surface types which have been classified as category 1 (slow pace) (see Appendix I).*

2. *Ball type 2 (medium) should only be used for play on court surface types which have been classified as category 2 (medium/medium-fast pace) (see Appendix I).*

3. *Ball type 3 (slow) should only be used for play on court surface types which have been classified as category 3 (fast pace) (see Appendix I).*

For non-professional play any ball type may be used on any surface type.

USTA Comment
Professional play refers to tournaments conducted under the regulations of the ATP Tour, ITF, and WTA Tour. This includes Satellite, Futures, and Challenger tournaments.

USTA Comment
For non-professional play, any ball type may be used in sanctioned tournaments if the ball has been approved by the ITF and the USTA. Because ball types 1 and 3 are authorized on an experimental basis only, results of matches played with ball type 1 or 3 count for ranking only if the applicable ranking regulations authorize the consideration of these matches.

---

4. THE RACKET

Rackets failing to comply with the following specifications

---

are not approved for play under the Rules of Tennis:

a. The hitting surface of the racket shall be flat and consist of a pattern of crossed strings connected to a frame and alternately interlaced or bonded where they cross; and the stringing pattern shall be generally uniform, and in particular not less dense in the centre than in any other area. The racket shall be designed and strung such that the playing characteristics are identical on both faces.

   The strings shall be free of attached objects and protrusions other than those utilised solely and specifically to limit or prevent wear and tear or vibration and which are reasonable in size and placement for such purposes.

b. The frame of the racket shall not exceed 29 inches (73.66cm.) in overall length, including the handle. The frame of the racket shall not exceed 12½ inches (31.75cm.) in overall width. The strung surface shall not exceed 15½ inches (39.37cm.) in overall length, and 11½ inches (29.21cm.) in overall width.

c. The frame, including the handle, shall be free of attached objects and devices other than those utilized solely and specifically to limit or prevent wear and tear or vibration, or to distribute weight. Any objects and devices must be reasonable in size and placement for such purposes.

d.   The frame, including the handle and the strings, shall be free of any device which makes it possible to change materially the shape of the racket, or to change the weight distribution in the direction of the longitudinal axis of the racket which would alter the swing moment of inertia, or to deliberately change any physical property which may affect the performance of the racket during the playing of a point.

   The International Tennis Federation shall rule on the question of whether any racket or prototype complies with the above specifications or is otherwise approved, or not approved, for play. Such ruling may be undertaken on its own initiative, or upon application by any party with a bona fide interest therein, including any player, equipment manufacturer or National Association or members thereof. Such rulings and applications shall be made in accordance with the applicable Review and Hearing Procedures of the International Tennis Federation (See Appendix II).

Case 1. Can there be more than one set of strings on the hitting surface of racket?
Decision. No. The rule clearly mentions a pattern, and not patterns, of crossed strings.

Case 2. Is the stringing pattern of a racket considered to be generally uniform and flat if the strings are on more than one plane?

Decision. No.

Case 3. Can vibration dampening devices be placed on the strings of a racket and if so, where can they be placed?

Decision. Yes; but such devices may be placed only outside the pattern of crossed strings.

Case 4. In the course of play, a player accidentally breaks the strings of his racket. Can he continue to play with the racket in this condition?

Decision. Yes

USTA Comment
If after play has begun it is discovered that a player has been using an illegal racket or an illegally strung racket, all points played stand. The player must find another racket immediately. If the discovery occurs after the match is over, the match still counts.

5. SERVER & RECEIVER

The players shall stand on opposite sides of the net; the player who first delivers the ball shall be called the Server, and the other the Receiver.

Case 1. Does a player, attempting a stroke, lose the point if he crosses an imaginary line in the extension of the net,

a. before striking the ball,

b. after striking the ball?

Decision. He does not lose the point in either case by crossing the imaginary line and provided he does not enter the lines bounding his opponent's Court [Rule 20(e)]. In regard to hindrance, his opponent may ask for the decision of the Umpire under Rules 21 and 25.

Case 2. The Server claims that the Receiver must stand within the lines bounding his Court. Is this necessary?
Decision. No. The Receiver may stand wherever he pleases on his own side of the net.

6. CHOICE OF ENDS & SERVICE

The choice of ends and the right to be Server or Receiver in the first game shall be decided by toss. The player winning the toss may choose or require his opponent to choose:

a. The right to be Server or Receiver, in which case the other player shall choose the end; or

b. The end, in which case the other player shall choose the right to be Server or Receiver.

Case 1. Do players have the right to new choices if the match is postponed or suspended before it has started?
Decision. Yes. The toss stands, but new choices may be made with respect to service and end.

USTA Comment
The toss shall be made before the warm-up. Choices should be made promptly after the toss and are irrevocable, except when the match is postponed or suspended before the start of the match.

---

7. THE SERVICE

The service shall be delivered in the following manner. Immediately before commencing to serve, the Server shall stand with both feet at rest behind (i.e. further from the net than) the base-line, and within the imaginary continuations of the centre-mark and side-line. The Server shall then project the ball by hand into the air in any direction and before it hits the ground strike it with his racket, and the delivery shall be deemed to have been completed at the moment of the impact of the racket and the ball. A player with the use of only one arm may utilize his racket for the projection.

USTA Comment
There is no restriction regarding the kind of service which may be used; that is, the player may use an underhand or overhand service at his discretion.

Case 1. May the Server in a singles game take his stand behind the portion of the base-line between the side-lines of the Singles Court and the Doubles Court?
Decision. No.

USTA Comment
In singles, the server may stand anywhere in back of the baseline between the imaginary extensions of the center mark and the singles sideline.

Case 2. If a player, when serving, throws up two or more balls instead of one, does he lose that service?
Decision. No. A let should be called, but if the Umpire regards the action as deliberate he may take ac-

tion under Rule 21.

8. FOOT FAULT

The Server shall throughout the delivery of the Service:

a. Not change his position by walking or running. The Server shall not by slight movement of the feet which do not materially affect the location originally taken up by him be deemed "to change his position by walking or running."

b. Not touch, with either foot, any area other than that behind the base-line within the imaginary extensions of the centre-mark and side-lines.

USTA Comment

The key to understanding this rule is to realize that the Server's feet must be at rest immediately before beginning to serve. Immediately thereafter, the delivery of the service begins with any arm or racket motion and ends when the racket contacts the ball (or misses the ball in attempt to strike it).

A player commits a foot fault if after his feet are at rest but before he strikes the ball, either foot touches:

- the Court, including the baseline;

- any part of the imaginary extension of the center mark; or

- beyond the imaginary extension of the outside edge of the sideline.

There can be no foot fault if the Server does not attempt to strike at the ball. As long as the Server makes no attempt to strike at the ball, it is immaterial whether he catches it in his hand or his racket or lets it drop to the

---

ground.

USTA Comment

This rule covers the most decisive stroke in the game, and there is no justification for its not being obeyed by players and enforced by officials. No official has the right to instruct any umpire to disregard violations of it. In a non-officiated match, the Receiver, or his partner, may call foot faults after all efforts (appeal to the server, request for an umpire, etc.) have failed and the foot faulting is so flagrant as to be clearly perceptible from the Receiver's side.

It is improper for any official to warn a player that he is in danger of having a foot fault called on him. On the other hand, if a player asks for an explanation of how he foot faulted, either the Line Umpire or the Chair Umpire should give him that information.

---

9. DELIVERY OF SERVICE

a. In delivering the service, the Server shall stand alternately behind the right and left halves of the Court beginning from the right in every game. If service from a wrong half of the Court occurs and is undetected, all play resulting from such wrong service or services shall stand, but the inaccuracy of station shall be corrected immediately when it is discovered.

b. The ball served shall pass over the net and hit the ground within the Service Court which is diagonally opposite or upon any line bounding such Court before the Receiver returns it.

---

10. SERVICE FAULT

The Service is a fault:

a.   If the Server commits any breach of Rules 7, 8 or 9(b);

b.   If he misses the ball in attempting to strike it;

c.   If the ball served touches a permanent fixture (other than the net, strap or band) before it hits the ground.

Case 1. After throwing a ball up preparatory to serving, the Server decides not to strike at it and catches it instead. Is it a fault?
Decision. No.

USTA Comment
As long as the Server makes no attempt to strike at the ball, it is immaterial whether he catches it in his hand or his racket or lets it drop to the ground.

Case 2. In serving in a singles game played on a Doubles Court with doubles posts and singles sticks, the ball hits a singles stick and then hits the ground within the lines of the correct Service Court. Is this a fault or a let?

Decision. In serving it is a fault, because the singles stick, the doubles post, and that portion of the net or band between them are permanent fixtures. (Rules 2 and 10, and note to Rule 24.)

USTA Comment
The significant point is that the part of the net and band "outside" the singles sticks is not part of the net over which this singles match is being played. Thus, such a serve is a fault under the provisions of subparagraph c. above. By the same token, this would be a fault also if it were a singles game played with permanent posts in the singles position. See Case 1 under Rule 24 for difference between "service" and "good return" with respect to a ball hitting a net post.

11. SECOND SERVICE

After a fault (if it is the first fault) the Server shall serve again from behind the same half of the Court from which he served that fault, unless the service was from the wrong half, when, in accordance with Rule 9, the Server shall be entitled to one service only from behind the other half.

Case 1. A player serves from a wrong Court. He loses the point and then claims it was a fault because of his wrong station.
Decision. The point stands as played and the next service should be from the correct station according to the score.

Case 2. The point score being 15 all, the Server, by mistake, serves from the left-hand Court. He wins the point. He then serves again from the right-hand Court, delivering a fault. This mistake in station is then discovered. Is he entitled to the previous point? From which Court should he next serve?

Decision. The previous point stands. The next service should be from the left-hand Court, the score being 30/15, and the Server having served one fault.

12. WHEN TO SERVE

The Server shall not serve until the Receiver is ready. If the latter attempts to return the service, he shall be deemed ready. If, however, the Receiver signifies that he is not ready, he may not claim a fault because the ball does not hit the ground within the limits fixed for the service.

USTA Comment
The Server must wait until the Receiver is ready for the second service as well as the first, and if the Receiver claims to be not ready and does not make any effort to return a service, the Server's claim for the point may not be honored even though the service was good. However, the Receiver, having indicated he is ready, may not become unready unless some outside interference takes place.

13. THE LET

In all cases where a let has to be called under the rules, or to provide for an interruption to play, it shall have the following interpretations:

a. When called solely in respect of a service, that one service only shall be replayed.

b. When called under any other circumstance, the point shall be replayed.

Case 1. A service is interrupted by some cause outside those defined in Rule 14. Should the service only be replayed?

Decision. No, the whole point must be replayed.

USTA Comment

If the interruption occurs during delivery of the second service, the Server gets two serves. Example: On a second service a linesman calls "fault" and immediately corrects it, the Receiver meanwhile having let the ball go by. The Server is entitled to two serves on this ground: The corrected call means that the Server has put the ball into play with a good service, and once the ball is in play and a let is called, the point must be replayed. Note, however, that if the serve is an unmistakable ace—that is, the Umpire is sure the erroneous call had no part in the Receiver's inability to play the ball—the point should be declared for the Server.

If a delay between first and second serves is caused by the Receiver, an official, or an outside interference, the whole point shall be replayed; if the delay is caused by the Server, the Server has one serve to come. A spectator's outcry (of "out," "fault," or other) is not a valid basis for replay of a point, but action should be taken to prevent a recurrence.

Case 2. If a ball in play becomes broken, should a let be called?

Decision. Yes

USTA Comment

A ball shall be regarded as having become "broken" if, in the opinion of the Umpire, it is found to have lost compression to the point of being unfit for further play, or unfit for any reason, and it is clear the defective ball was the one in play.

---

14. THE "LET" IN SERVICE

The Service is a let:

a.   If the ball served touches the net, strap or band, and is otherwise good, or, after touching the net, strap or band, touches the Receiver or anything which he wears or carries before hitting the ground.

b.   If a service or a fault is delivered when the Receiver is not ready (see Rule 12).

In case of a let, that particular service shall not count, and the Server shall serve again, but a service let does not annul a previous fault.

15. ORDER OF SERVICE

At the end of the first game, the Receiver shall become Server, and the Server Receiver; and so on alternately in all the subsequent games of a match. If a player serves out of turn, the player who ought to have served shall serve as soon as the mistake is discovered, but all points scored before such discovery shall stand. A fault served before such discovery shall not stand. If a game shall have been completed before such discovery, the order of service shall remain as altered.

16. WHEN PLAYERS CHANGE ENDS

The players shall change ends at the end of the first, third and every subsequent alternate game of each set, and at the end of each set unless the total number of games in such set is even, in which case the change is not made until the end of the first game of the next set.

If a mistake is made and the correct sequence is not followed the players must take up their correct station as soon as the discovery is made and follow their original sequence.

17. THE BALL IN PLAY

A ball is in play from the moment at which it is delivered in service. Unless a fault or a let is called it remains in play until the point is decided.

> ### USTA Comment
> A point is not decided simply when, or because, a good shot has clearly passed a player, or when an apparently bad shot passes over a baseline or sideline. An outgoing ball is still definitely in play until it actually strikes the ground, backstop, a permanent fixture (other than the net, posts, singles sticks, cord or metal cable, strap or band), or a player. The same applies to a good ball, bounding after it has landed in the proper Court. A ball that becomes imbedded in the net is out of play.

> ### USTA Comment
> When a ball is hit into the net and the player on the other side, thinking the ball is coming over, strikes at it and hits the net he loses the point if his touching the net occurs while the ball is still in play.

Case 1. A player fails to make a good return. No call is made and the ball remains in play. May his opponent later claim the point after the rally has ended?
Decision. No. The point may not be claimed if the

players continue to play after the error has been made, provided the opponent was not hindered.

USTA Comment

An out call on A's shot to B's Court must be made before B's return has either gone out of play or been hit by A. See Case 3 under Rule 29 regarding this situation in an umpired match.

18. SERVER WINS POINT

The Server wins the point:

a.   If the ball served, not being a let under Rule 14, touches the Receiver or anything which he wears or carries, before it hits the ground;

b.   If the Receiver otherwise loses the point as provided by Rule 20.

19. RECEIVER WINS POINT

The Receiver wins the point:

a.   If the Server serves two consecutive faults;

b.   If the Server otherwise loses the point as provided by Rule 20.

20. PLAYER LOSES POINT

A player loses the point if:

a.   He fails, before the ball in play has hit the ground twice consecutively, to return it directly over the net [except as provided in Rule 24(a) or (c)]; or

b. He returns the ball in play so that it hits the ground, a permanent fixture, or other object, outside any of the lines which bound his opponent's Court; or

c. He volleys the ball and fails to make a good return even when standing outside the Court; or

---

USTA Comment
A ball hitting a scoring device or other object attached to a net post results in loss of point to the striker.

---

d. In playing the ball he deliberately carries or catches it on his racket or deliberately touches it with his racket more than once; or

---

USTA Comment
Only when there is a definite "second push" by the player does his shot become illegal, with consequent loss of point. The word "deliberately" is the key word in this rule. Two hits occurring in the course of a single continuous swing are not deemed a double hit.

---

e. He or his racket (in his hand or otherwise) or anything which he wears or carries touches the net, posts, singles sticks, cord or metal cable, strap or band, or the ground within his opponent's Court at any time while the ball is in play; or

---

USTA Comment
Touching a pipe support that runs across the Court at the bottom of the net is interpreted as touching the net. See USTA Comment under Rule 23 for a ball which hits a pipe support.

f. He volleys the ball before it has passed the net; or

g. The ball in play touches him or anything that he wears or carries, except his racket in his hand or hands; or

USTA Comment
This loss of point occurs regardless of whether the player is inside or outside the bounds of his Court when the ball touches him.

h. He throws his racket at and hits the ball; or

i. He deliberately and materially changes the shape of his racket during the playing of the point.

Case 1. In serving, the racket flies from the Server's hand and touches the net before the ball has touched the ground. Is this a fault, or does the player lose the point?
Decision. The Server loses the point because his racket touches the net whilst the ball is in play [Rule 20(e)].

Case 2. In serving, the racket flies from the Server's hand and touches the net after the ball has touched the ground outside the proper court. Is this a fault, or does the player lose the point?

Decision. This is a fault because the ball was out of play when the racket touched the net.

Case 3. A and B are playing against C and D, A is serving to D, C touches the net before the ball touches the ground. A fault is then called because the service falls outside the Service Court. Do C and D lose the point?

Decision. The call "fault" is an erroneous one. C and D had already lost the point before "fault" could be called, because C touched the net whilst the ball was in play [Rule 20(e)].

Case 4. May a player jump over the net into his opponent's Court while the ball is in play and not suffer penalty?

Decision. No. He loses the point [Rule 20(e)].

Case 5. A cuts the ball just over the net, and it returns to A's side. B, unable to reach the ball, throws his racket and hits the ball. Both racket and ball fall over the net on A's Court. A returns the ball outside of B's Court. Does B win or lose the point?

Decision. B loses the point [Rule 20(e) and (h)].

Case 6. A player standing outside the service Court is struck by a service ball before it has touched the ground. Does he win or lose the point?

Decision. The player struck loses the point [Rule 20(g)], except as provided under Rule 14(a).

Case 7. A player standing outside the Court volleys the ball or catches it in his hand and claims the point because the ball was certainly going out of court.

Decision. In no circumstances can he claim the point:

   i. If he catches the ball he loses the point under Rule 20(g).

   ii. If he volleys it and makes a bad return he loses the point under Rule 20(c).

   iii. If he volleys it and makes a good return, the rally continues.

21. PLAYER HINDERS OPPONENT

If a player commits any act which hinders his opponent in making a stroke, then, if this is deliberate, he shall lose the point or if involuntary, the point shall be replayed.

Case 1. Is a player liable to a penalty if in making a stroke he touches his opponent?

Decision. No, unless the Umpire deems it necessary to take action under Rule 21.

Case 2. When a ball bounds back over the net, the player concerned may reach over the net in order to play the ball. What is the ruling if the player is hindered from doing this by his opponent?

Decision. In accordance with Rule 21, the Umpire may either award the point to the player hindered, or order the point to be replayed (see also Rule 25).

Case 3. Does an involuntary double hit constitute an

act which hinders an opponent within Rule 21?
Decision. No.

USTA Comment

"Deliberate" means a player did what he intended to do, although the resulting effect on his opponent might or might not have been what he intended. Example: A player, after his return is in the air, gives advice to his partner in such a loud voice that his opponent is hindered. "Involuntary" means a non-intentional act such as a hat blowing off or a scream resulting from a sudden wasp sting.

---

22. BALL FALLS ON LINE

A ball falling on a line is regarded as falling in the Court bounded by that line.

USTA Comment

In a non-officiated match, each player makes the call on any ball hit toward his side of the net. If a player cannot call a ball out with certainty, he should regard it as good. In doubles, normally the Receiver's partner makes the calls with respect to the service line, with the Receiver calling the side and center lines, but either partner may make the call on any ball he clearly sees out.

---

23. BALL TOUCHES PERMANENT FIXTURES

If the ball in play touches a permanent fixture (other than the net, posts, singles sticks, cord or metal cable, strap or band) after it has hit the ground, the player who struck it wins the point; if before it hits the ground, his opponent

---

wins the point.

USTA Comment

A ball in play that strikes a pipe support running across the Court at the base of the net is treated the same as a ball landing on clear ground. See USTA Comment under Rule 20(e) for a player who touches a pipe support.

Case 1. A return hits the Umpire or his chair or stand. The player claims that the ball was going into Court.

Decision. He loses the point.

24. A GOOD RETURN

It is a good return:

a.   If the ball touches the net, posts, singles sticks, cord or metal cable, strap or band, provided that it passes over any of them and hits the ground within the Court; or

b.   If the ball, served or returned, hits the ground within the proper Court and rebounds or is blown back over the net, and the player whose turn it is to strike reaches over the net and plays the ball, provided that he does not contravene Rule 20(e); or

c.   If the ball is returned outside the posts or singles sticks, either above or below the level of the top of the net, even though it touches the posts or singles sticks, provided that it hits the ground within the proper Court; or

---

d.   If a player's racket passes over the net after he has returned the ball, provided the ball passes the net before being played and is properly returned; or

e.   If a player succeeds in returning the ball, served or in play, which strikes a ball lying in the Court.

USTA Comment

Paragraph e. of the rule refers to a ball lying on the Court at the start of the point as a result of a service let or fault or as a result of a player dropping it. If a ball in play strikes a rolling or stationary "foreign" ball that has come from elsewhere after the point started, a let should be played. See Case 7 under Rule 25 which pertains to an object other than a ball that is being used in the match.

ITF Note: In a singles match, if, for the sake of convenience, a Doubles Court is equipped with singles sticks for the purpose of a singles game, then the doubles posts and those portions of the net, cord or metal cable and the band outside such singles sticks shall at all times be permanent fixtures, and are not regarded as posts or parts of the net of a singles game.

A return that passes under the net cord between the singles stick and adjacent doubles post without touching either net cord, net or doubles post and falls within the court is a good return.

USTA Comment

In doubles this would be a "through"—loss of point.

Case 1. A ball going out of Court hits a net post or

singles stick and falls within the lines of the opponent's Court. Is the stroke good?

Decision. If a service: no, under Rule 10(c). If other than a service: yes, under Rule 24(a).

Case 2. Is it a good return if a player returns the ball holding his racket in both hands?

Decision. Yes.

Case 3. The service, or ball in play, strikes a ball lying in the Court. Is the point won or lost thereby?

Decision. No. Play must continue. If it is not clear to the Umpire that the right ball is returned a let should be called.

USTA Comment
A ball that is touching a boundary line is considered to be "lying in the Court."

Case 4. May a player use more than one racket at any time during play?

Decision. No. The whole implication of the Rules is singular.

Case 5. May a player request that a ball or balls lying in his opponent's Court be removed?

Decision. Yes, but not while a ball is in play.

USTA Comment
This request must be honored.

---

25. HINDRANCE OF A PLAYER

In case a player is hindered in making a stroke by anything not within his control, except a permanent fixture of the Court, or except as provided for in Rule 21, a let shall be called.

USTA Comment
See Rule 13 and its USTA Comments regarding lets.

Case 1. A spectator gets into the way of a player, who fails to return the ball. May the player then claim a let?
Decision. Yes, if in the Umpire's opinion he was obstructed by circumstances beyond his control, but not if due to permanent fixtures of the Court or the arrangements of the ground.

Case 2. A player is interfered with as in Case No.1, and the Umpire calls a let. The Server had previously served a fault. Has he the right to two services?
Decision. Yes. If the ball is in play, the point, not merely the stroke, must be replayed as the Rule provides.

Case 3. May a player claim a let under Rule 25 because he thought his opponent was being hindered, and consequently did not expect the ball to be returned?
Decision. No.

Case 4. Is a stroke good when a ball in play hits another ball in the air?

Decision. A let should be called unless the other ball is in the air by the act of one of the players, in which case the Umpire will decide under Rule 21.

Case 5. If an Umpire or other judge erroneously calls "fault" or "out" and then corrects himself, which of the calls shall prevail?
Decision. A let must be called unless, in the opinion of the Umpire, neither player is hindered in his game, in which case the corrected call shall prevail.

Case 6. If the first ball served—a fault—rebounds, interfering with the Receiver at the time of the second service, may the Receiver claim a let?
Decision. Yes. But if he had an opportunity to remove the ball from the Court and negligently failed to do so, he may not claim a let.

Case 7. Is it a good stroke if the ball touches a stationary or moving object on the Court?
Decision. It is a good stroke unless the stationary object came into Court after the ball was put into play in which case a let must be called. If the ball in play strikes an object moving along or above the surface of the Court a let must be called.

Case 8. What is the ruling if the first service is a fault, the second service correct, and it becomes necessary to call a let either under the provision of Rule 25 or if the Umpire is unable to decide the point?
Decision. The fault shall be annulled and the whole point replayed.

26. SCORE IN A GAME

a. If a player wins his first point, the score is called 15 for that player; on winning his second point, the score is called 30 for that player; on winning his third point, the score is called 40 for that player, and the fourth point won by a player is scored game for that player except as below:

    If both players have won three points, the score is called deuce; and the next point won by a player is scored advantage for that player. If the same player wins the next point, he wins the game; if the other player wins the next point the score is again called deuce; and so on, until a player wins the two points immediately following the score at deuce, when the game is scored for that player.

b. Optional Alternative Scoring System

    The No-Ad System of Scoring may be adopted as an alternative to the traditional scoring system during the period 1 January 1999 to 31 December 2000 provided the decision is announced in advance of the event.

    In this case, the following Rules shall be effective:

    If a player wins his first point, the score is called 15 for that player; on winning his second point, the score is called 30 for that player; on winning his third point, the score is called 40 for that player, and the fourth point won by a player is scored game for that player except as below:

If both players have won three points, the score is called deuce; one deciding point shall then be played whereby the receiver shall choose whether he wishes to receive the service from the right-half of the court or the left-half of the court. The player who wins the deciding point is scored the game.

Doubles

In doubles a similar procedure to that for singles shall apply. At deuce the Receiving Team shall choose whether it wishes to receive the Service from the right-half of the court or the left-half of the court. The team who wins the deciding point is scored the game.

Mixed Doubles

In mixed doubles, a slightly different procedure will apply as follows: At deuce, with the male player serving, he shall serve to the male player of the opposing team irrespective of which half of the court he is standing, and when the female player is serving, she shall serve to the female player of the opposing team.

USTA Comment

In a non-officiated match the Server should announce, in a voice audible to his opponent and spectators, the set score at the beginning of each game, and point scores as the game goes on. Misunderstandings will be avoided if this practice is followed.

27. SCORE IN A SET

a. A player (or players) who first wins six games wins a set; except that he must win by a margin of two games over his opponent and where necessary a set is extended until this margin is achieved.

b. The tie-break system of scoring may be adopted as an alternative to the advantage set system in paragraph (a) of this Rule provided the decision is announced in advance of the match.

In this case, the following Rules shall be effective: The tie-break shall operate when the score reaches six games all in any set except in the third or fifth set of a three-set or five-set match respectively when an ordinary advantage set shall be played, unless otherwise decided and announced in advance of the match.

The following system shall be used in a tie-break game:

Singles

i. A player who first wins seven points shall win the game and the set provided he leads by a margin of two points. If the score reaches six points all the game shall be extended until this margin has been achieved. Numerical scoring shall be used throughout the tie-break game.

ii. The player whose turn it is to serve shall be the Server for the first point. His opponent shall be the Server for the second and third points and thereafter each player shall serve alternately for two consecutive points until the winner of the game and set has been decided.

iii. From the first point, each service shall be delivered alternately from the right and left Courts, beginning from the right Court. If service from a wrong half of the Court occurs and is undetected, all play resulting from such wrong service or services shall stand, but the inaccuracy of station shall be corrected immediately when it is discovered.

iv. Players shall change ends after every six points and at the conclusion of the tie-break game.

v. The tie-break game shall count as one game for the ball change, except that, if the balls are due to be changed at the beginning of the tie-break, the change shall be delayed until the second game of the following set.

Doubles

In doubles the procedure for singles shall apply. The player whose turn it is to serve shall be the Server for the first point. Thereafter each player shall serve in rotation for two points, in the same order previously in that set, until the winners of the game and set have been decided.

Rotation of Service

The player (or pair in the case of doubles) whose turn it was to serve first in the tie-break game shall receive service in the first game of the following set.

> **Case 1.** At six all the tie-break is played, although it has been decided and announced in advance of the match that an advantage set will be played. Are the points already played counted?
>
> **Decision.** If the error is discovered before the ball is put in play for the second point, the first point shall count but the error shall be corrected immediately. If the error is discovered after the ball is put in play for the second point the game shall continue as a tie-break game.
>
> **Case 2.** At six all, an advantage game is played, although it has been decided and announced in advance of the match that a tie-break will be played. Are the points already played counted?
>
> **Decision.** If the error is discovered before the ball is put in play for the second point, the first point shall be counted but the error shall be corrected immediately. If the error is discovered after the ball is put in play for the second point an advantage set shall be continued. If the score thereafter reaches eight games all or a higher even number, a tie-break shall be played.

Case 3. If during a tie-break in a singles or doubles game a player serves out of turn, shall the order of service remain as altered until the end of the game?

Decision. If a player has completed his turn of service the order of service shall remain as altered. If the error is discovered before a player has completed his turn of service the order of service shall be corrected immediately and any points already played shall count.

28. MAXIMUM NUMBER OF SETS

The maximum number of sets in a match shall be 5, or, where women take part, 3.

29. ROLE OF COURT OFFICIALS

In matches where an Umpire is appointed, his decision shall be final; but where a Referee is appointed, an appeal shall lie to him from the decision of an Umpire on a question of law, and in all such cases the decision of the Referee shall be final.

In matches where assistants to the Umpire are appointed (Linespersons, Net-cord Judges, Foot-fault Judges) their decisions shall be final on questions of fact except that if in the opinion of an Umpire a clear mistake has been made he shall have the right to change the decision of an assistant or order a let to be played. When such an assistant is unable to give a decision he shall indicate this immediately to the Umpire who shall give a decision. When an Umpire is unable to give a decision on a question of fact he shall order a let to be played.

In Davis Cup matches or other team competitions where a Referee is on Court, any decision can be changed by the Referee, who may also instruct an Umpire to order a let to be played.

The Referee, in his discretion, may at any time postpone a match on account of darkness or the condition of the ground or the weather. In any case of postponement the previous score and previous occupancy of courts shall hold good, unless the Referee and the players unanimously agree otherwise.

USTA Comment
See fourth USTA Comment under Rule 30 regarding resumption of suspended match.

Case 1. The Umpire orders a let, but a player claims that the point should not be replayed. May the Referee be requested to give a decision?
Decision. Yes. A question of tennis law, that is, an issue relating to the application of specific facts, shall first be determined by the Umpire. However, if the Umpire is uncertain or if a player appeals from his determination, then the Referee shall be requested to give a decision, and his decision is final.

Case 2. A ball is called out, but a player claims that the ball was good. May the Referee give a ruling?
Decision. No. This is a question of fact, that is an issue relating to what actually occurred during a specific incident, and the decision of the on-court officials is therefore final.

Case 3. May an Umpire overrule a Linesman at the end of a rally if, in his opinion, a clear mistake has been made during the course of a rally?

Decision. No. An Umpire may overrule a Linesman only if he does so immediately after the mistake has been made.

USTA Comment
See Rule 17, Case 1, regarding non-officiated matches.

Case 4. A Linesman calls a ball out. The Umpire was unable to see clearly, although he thought the ball was in. May he overrule the Linesman?

Decision. No. An Umpire may only overrule if he considers that a call was incorrect beyond all reasonable doubt. He may only overrule a ball determined good by a Linesman only if he has been able to see a space between the ball and the line; and he may only overrule a ball determined out, or a fault, by a Linesman only if he has seen the ball hit the line, or fall inside the line.

Case 5. May a Linesman change his call after the Umpire has given the score?

Decision. Yes. If a Linesman realises he has made an error, he may make a correction provided he does so immediately.

Case 6. A player claims his return shot was good after a Linesman called "out." May the Umpire overrule the Linesman?

Decision. No. An Umpire may never overrule as a result of a protest or an appeal by a player.

30. CONTINUOUS PLAY & REST PERIODS

Play shall be continuous from the first service until the match is concluded, in accordance with the following provisions:

a. If the first service is a fault, the second service must be struck by the Server without delay.

    The Receiver must play to the reasonable pace of the Server and must be ready to receive when the Server is ready to serve.

    When changing ends a maximum of one minute thirty seconds shall elapse from the moment the ball goes out of play at the end of the game to the time the ball is struck for the first point of the next game.

    The Umpire shall use his discretion when there is interference which makes it impractical for play to be continuous.

    The organisers of international circuits and team events recognised by the ITF may determine the time allowed between points, which shall not at any time exceed twenty (20) seconds from the moment the ball goes out of play at the end of one point to the time the ball is struck for the next point.

USTA Comment

The 20-second rule applies only to certain international circuits and team events recognized by the ITF. When practical, in USTA sanctioned tournaments using a certified official in direct observation of the match, the time which shall elapse from the moment the ball goes out of play at the end of the point to the time the ball is struck shall not exceed 25 seconds.

b. Play shall never be suspended, delayed or interfered with for the purpose of enabling a player to recover his strength, breath, or physical condition.

   However, in the case of a treatable medical condition, the Umpire may allow a one-time three minute suspension for that injury.

c. If, through circumstances outside the control of the player, his clothing, footwear or equipment (excluding racket) becomes out of adjustment in such a way that it is impossible or undesirable for him to play on, the Umpire may suspend play while the maladjustment is rectified.

USTA Comment

If equipment other than a racket becomes unusable through circumstances outside the control of the player, play may be suspended for a reasonable period and the player may leave the Court to correct the problem. If a racket or racket string is broken, Rule 30 does not permit play to be suspended. A player who leaves the Court to get a replacement is subject to code violation(s) under the Point Penalty System.

USTA Comment
Loss of, or damage to, a contact lens or eyeglasses shall be treated as equipment maladjustment. All players must follow the same rules with respect to suspending play, even though in misty but playable weather, a player who wears glasses may be handicapped.

d. The Umpire may suspend or delay play at any time as may be necessary and appropriate.

e. After the third set, or when women take part the second set, either player is entitled to a rest, which shall not exceed 10 minutes, or in countries situated between latitude 15 degrees north and latitude 15 degrees south, 45 minutes and furthermore, when necessitated by circumstances not within the control of the players, the Umpire may suspend play for such a period as he may consider necessary. If play is suspended and is not resumed until a later day the rest may be taken only after the third set (or when women take part the second set) of play on such a later day, completion of an unfinished set being counted as one set.

   If play is suspended and is not resumed until 10 minutes have elapsed in the same day the rest may be taken only after three consecutive sets have been played without interruption (or when women take part two sets), completion of an unfinished set being counted as one set.

   Any nation and/or committee organising a tournament, match or competition, is at liberty to modify this provision or omit it from its regulations provided this is announced before the event commences. With respect to the Davis Cup and Fed Cup, only the International Tennis Federation may modify this provision or omit it from its Regulations.

USTA Comment
When a match is resumed after a suspension of more than ten minutes, it is permissible for the players to engage in a re-warm-up that may be of the same duration as that at the start of the match. The preferred method is to warm-up with other used balls and then insert the match balls when play starts. If the match balls are used in the re-warm-up, then the next ball change will be two games sooner. There shall be no re-warm-up after an authorized intermission or after a suspension of ten minutes or less.

f. A tournament committee has the discretion to decide the time allowed for a warm-up period prior to a match but this may not exceed five minutes and must be announced before the event commences.

USTA Comment
When there are no ballpersons, this time may be extended to 10 minutes.

g. When approved point penalty and non-accumulative point penalty systems are in operation, the Umpire shall make his decisions within the terms of those systems.

h. Upon violation of the principle that play shall be continuous the Umpire may, after giving due warning, disqualify the offender.

31. COACHING

During the playing of a match in a team competition, a player may receive coaching from a captain who is sitting on the court only when he changes ends at the end of a game, but not when he changes ends during a tie-break game.

A player may not receive coaching during the playing of any other match. The provisions of this rule must be strictly construed.

After due warning an offending player may be disqualified. When an approved point penalty system is in operation, the Umpire shall impose penalties according to that system.

Case 1. Should a warning be given, or the player be disqualified, if the coaching is given by signals in an unobtrusive manner?

Decision. The Umpire must take action as soon as he becomes aware that coaching is being given verbally or by signals. If the Umpire is unaware that coaching is being given, a player may draw his attention to the fact that advice is being given.

Case 2. Can a player receive coaching during an authorised rest period under Rule 30(e), or when play is interrupted and he leaves the court?

Decision. Yes. In these circumstances, when the

player is not on the court, there is no restriction on coaching.

USTA Comment
Coaching is not permitted in the USA Adult and Senior League Program except during authorized rest periods.

USTA Comment
No player may receive coaching during a toilet visit.

ITF Note: The word "coaching" includes any advice or instruction.

32. BALL CHANGE

In cases where balls are to be changed after a specified number of games, if the balls are not changed in the correct sequence, the mistake shall be corrected when the player, or pair in the case of doubles, who should have served with new balls is next due to serve. Thereafter the balls shall be changed so that the number of games between changes shall be that originally agreed.

The
Doubles
Game

USTA

33. THE DOUBLES GAME

The above Rules shall apply to the Doubles Game except as below.

34. THE DOUBLES COURT

For the Doubles Game, the court shall be 36 feet (10.97m.) in width, i.e. 4½ feet (1.37m.) wider on each side than the Court for the Singles Game, and those portions of the singles side-lines which lie between the two service-lines shall be called the service side-lines. In other respects, the Court shall be similar to that described in Rule 1, but the portions of the singles side-lines between the base-line and service-line on each side of the net may be omitted if desired.

USTA Comment
The Server has the right in doubles to stand anywhere in back of the baseline between the center mark imaginary extension and the doubles sideline imaginary extension.

35. ORDER OF SERVICE IN DOUBLES

The order of serving shall be decided at the beginning of each set as follows:

The pair who have to serve in the first game of each set shall decide which partner shall do so and the opposing pair shall decide similarly for the second game. The partner of the player who served in the first game shall serve in the third; the partner of the player who served in the second game shall serve in the fourth, and so on in the same order in all the subsequent games of a set.

Case 1. In doubles, one player does not appear in time to play, and his partner claims to be allowed to play single-handed against the opposing players. May he do so?

Decision. No.

36. ORDER OF RECEIVING IN DOUBLES

The order of receiving the service shall be decided at the beginning of each set as follows:

The pair who have to receive the service in the first game shall decide which partner shall receive the first service, and that partner shall continue to receive the first service in every odd game throughout that set. The opposing pair shall likewise decide which partner shall receive the first service in the second game and that partner shall continue to receive the first service in every even game throughout that set. Partners shall receive the service alternately throughout each game.

Case 1. Is it allowable in doubles for the Server's partner or the Receiver's partner to stand in a position that obstructs the view of the Receiver?

Decision. Yes. The Server's partner or the Receiver's partner may take any position on his side of the net in or out of the Court that he wishes.

37. SERVICE OUT OF TURN IN DOUBLES

If a partner serves out of his turn, the partner who ought to have served shall serve as soon as the mistake is discovered, but all points scored, and any faults served before such discovery, shall be reckoned. If a game shall have been completed before such discovery, the order of service remains as altered.

USTA Comment
For an exception to Rule 37, see Case 3 under Rule 27.

---

38. ERROR IN ORDER OF RECEIVING IN DOUBLES

If during a game the order of receiving the service is changed by the Receivers it shall remain as altered until the end of the game in which the mistake is discovered, but the partners shall resume their original order of receiving in the next game of that set in which they are Receivers of the service.

39. SERVICE FAULT IN DOUBLES

The service is a fault as provided for by Rule 10, or if the ball touches the Server's partner or anything which he wears or carries; but if the ball served touches the partner of the Receiver, or anything which he wears or carries, not being a let under Rule 14(a) before it hits the ground, the Server wins the point.

40. PLAYING THE BALL IN DOUBLES

The ball shall be struck alternately by one or other player of the opposing pairs, and if a player touches the ball in play with his racket in contravention of this Rule, his opponents win the point.

ITF Note 1: Except where otherwise stated, every reference in these Rules to the masculine includes the feminine gender.

ITF Note 2: See Rule 26(b) with regard to the Optional Alternative Scoring System in Doubles and Mixed.

USTA Comment
The partners themselves do not have to "alternate" in making returns. In the course of making one return, only one member of a doubles team may hit the ball. If both of them hit the ball, either simultaneously or consecutively, it is an illegal return. Mere clashing of rackets does not make a return illegal unless it is clear that more than one racket touched the ball.

Rules of Wheelchair Tennis

The game of wheelchair tennis follows the same rules as able-bodied tennis as endorsed by the International Tennis Federation except the wheelchair tennis player is allowed two bounces of the ball. The player must return the ball before it hits the ground a third time. The wheelchair is part of the body and all applicable ITF Rules which apply to a player's body shall apply to the wheelchair.

I. THE COMPETITIVE WHEELCHAIR TENNIS PLAYER

a. In order to be eligible to compete in sanctioned ITF wheelchair tennis tournaments and the paralympic games, a player must have a medically diagnosed permanent mobility-related physical disability. This permanent physical disability must result in a substantial or total loss of function in one or more lower extremities. If, as a result of these functional limitations, the player is unable to play competitive able-bodied tennis (that is, having the mobility to cover the court with adequate speed), then the player is eligible to play competitive wheelchair tennis in sanctioned ITF wheelchair tennis tournaments.

b. Examples of permanent disabilities that meet the eligibility criteria are: paralysis; amputation; radiological evidence of limb shortening; partial to full joint ankylosis or joint replacement. Such physical disabilities must consistently interfere with functional mobility. Findings such as soft tissue contracture, ligamentous instability, edema or disuse atrophy, or symptoms such as pain or numbness, without other eligibility criteria listed above shall not be considered a permanent physical disability.

c. A quadriplegic division player shall be characterised as one who meets the criteria for permanent physical disability as defined above in at least three extremities.

Any questions or appeal as to a player's eligibility to participate under this rule will be decided under the procedures listed in Appendix III.

II. THE SERVICE

a. The served ball may, after hitting the ground in the service court, hit the ground once again within the bounds of the court or it may hit the ground outside the court boundaries before the receiver returns it.

b. The service shall be delivered in the following manner: Immediately before commencing to serve, the server shall be in a stationary position. The server shall then be allowed one push before striking the ball.

c. The server shall throughout the delivery of the service not touch, with any wheel, any area other than that behind the baseline within the imaginary extension of the centre mark and sideline.

d. If conventional methods for the service are physically impossible for a quadriplegic player, then such a player or another individual may drop the ball for such player. However, the same method of serving must be used each time.

III. THE BALL IN PLAY

The ball is in play until the point is decided. The ball must be returned into the opponent's court prior to it touching the ground a third time. The second bounce can be either in or out of the court boundaries.

IV. PLAYER LOSES POINT

A player loses a point if:

a. He fails to return the ball before it has touched the ground three times.

b. He uses any part of his feet or lower extremities against the ground or against any wheel while the ball is in play.

c. He fails to keep one buttock in contact with his wheelchair seat when contacting the ball.

V. WHEELCHAIR/ABLE-BODIED TENNIS

Where a wheelchair player as defined in Rule I above is playing with or against an able-bodied person in singles or in doubles, the rules of wheelchair tennis shall apply for the wheelchair player while the Rules of Tennis for able-bodied tennis shall apply for the able-bodied player. In this instance, the wheelchair player is allowed two bounces while the able-bodied player is allowed only one bounce.

> ***ITF Note:*** *The definition of lower extremities is: the lower limb, including the buttocks, hip, thigh, leg, ankle, and foot.*

The
Code

THE PLAYERS' GUIDE
FOR UNOFFICIATED MATCHES
2000

PREFACE

When your serve hits your partner stationed at the net, is it a let, fault, or loss of point? Likewise, what is the ruling when your serve, before touching the ground, hits an opponent who is standing *back* of the baseline? The answers to these questions are obvious to anyone who knows the fundamentals of tennis, but it is surprising the number of players who don't know these fundamentals. All players have a responsibility to be familiar with the basic rules and customs of tennis. Further, it can be distressing to your opponent when he makes a decision in accordance with a rule and you protest with the remark: "Well, I never heard of that rule before!" Ignorance of the rules constitutes a delinquency on the part of a player and often spoils an otherwise good match.

What is written here constitutes the essentials of *The Code,* a summary of procedures and unwritten rules which custom and tradition dictate all players should follow. No system of rules will cover every specific problem or situation that may arise. If players of goodwill follow the principles of *The Code,* they should always be able to reach an agreement, while at the same time making tennis more fun and a better game for all. The principles set forth in *The Code* shall apply in cases not specifically covered by The Rules of Tennis and USTA Regulations.

Before reading this you might well ask yourself: Since we have a book that contains all the rules of tennis, why do we need a code? Isn't it sufficient to know and understand all the rules? There are a number of things not specifically set forth in the rules that are covered by custom and tradition only. For example, if you have a doubt on a line call, your opponent gets the benefit of the doubt. Can you find that in the rules? Further, custom dictates the standard procedures that players will use in reaching decisions. These are the reasons why we need a code.

—Col. Nick Powel

Note: This edition of The Code is an adaptation of the original, which was written by Colonel Nicholas E. Powel.

PRINCIPLES

1. *Courtesy.* Tennis is a game that requires cooperation and courtesy from all participants. Make tennis a fun game by praising your opponents' good shots and by not:

    • conducting loud postmortems after points;

    • complaining about shots like lobs and drop shots;

    • embarrassing a weak opponent by being overly gracious or condescending;

    • losing your temper, using vile language, throwing your racket, or slamming a ball in anger; or

    • sulking when you are losing.

2.   *Counting points played in good faith.* All points played in good faith stand. For example, if after losing a point, a player discovers that the net was four inches too high, the point stands. If a point is played from the wrong court, there is no replay. If during a point, a player realizes that a mistake was made at the beginning (for example, service from the wrong court), he shall continue playing the point. Corrective action may be taken only after a point has been completed.

THE WARM-UP

3.   *Warm-up is not practice.* A player should provide his opponent a five-minute warm-up (ten minutes if there are no ball persons). If a player refuses to warm-up his opponent, he forfeits his right to a warm-up. Some players confuse warm-up and practice. A player should make a special effort to hit his shots directly to his opponent. (If partners want to warm each other up while their opponents are warming up, they may do so.)

4.   *Warm-up serves.* Take all your warm-up serves before the first serve of the match. Courtesy dictates that you not practice your service return when your opponent practices his serve. If a player has completed his warm-up serves, he shall return warm-up serves directly to his opponent.

MAKING CALLS

5. *Player makes calls on his side of the net.* A player calls all shots landing on, or aimed at, his side of the net.

6. *Opponent gets benefit of doubt.* When a match is played without officials, the players are responsible for making decisions, particularly for line calls. There is a subtle difference between player decisions and those of an on-court official. An official impartially resolves a problem involving a call, whereas a player is guided by the unwritten law that any doubt must be resolved in favor of his opponent. A player in attempting to be scrupulously honest on line calls frequently will find himself keeping a ball in play that might have been out or that he discovers too late was out. *Even so, the game is much better played this way.*

7. *Ball touching any part of line is good.* If any part of the ball touches the line, the ball is good. A ball 99% out is still 100% good.

8. *Ball that cannot be called out is good.* Any ball that cannot be called out is considered to have been good. A player may not claim a let on the basis that he did not see a ball. One of tennis' most infuriating moments occurs after a long hard rally when a player makes a clean placement and his opponent says: "I'm not sure if it was good or out. Let's play a let." Remember, it is each player's responsibility to call all balls landing on, or aimed at, his side of the net. If a ball can't be

called out with certainty, it is good. When you say your opponent's shot was really out but you offer to replay the point to give him a break, you are deluding yourself because you must have had some doubt.

9. *Calls when looking across a line or when far away.* The call of a player looking down a line is much more likely to be accurate than that of a player looking across a line. When you are looking across a line, don't call a ball out unless you can clearly see part of the court between where the ball hit and the line. It is difficult for a player who stands on one baseline to question a call on a ball that landed near the other baseline.

10. *Treat all points the same regardless of their importance.* All points in a match should be treated the same. There is no justification for considering a match point differently than the first point.

11. *Requesting opponent's help.* When an opponent's opinion is requested and he gives a positive opinion, it must be accepted. If neither player has an opinion, the ball is considered good. Aid from an opponent is available only on a call that ends a point.

12. *Out calls corrected.* If a player mistakenly calls a ball "out" and then realizes it was good, the point shall be replayed if he returned the ball within the proper court. Nonetheless, if the player's return of the ball results in a "weak sitter," the player should give his

opponent the point. If the player failed to make the return, his opponent wins the point. If the mistake was made on the second serve, the server is entitled to two serves.

13. *Player calls his own shots out.* With the exception of the first serve, a player should call against himself any ball he clearly sees out regardless of whether he is requested to do so by his opponent. The prime objective in making calls is accuracy. All players should cooperate to attain this objective.

14. *Partners' disagreement on calls.* If a player and his partner disagree about whether their opponents' ball was out, they shall call it good. It is more important to give your opponents the benefit of the doubt than to avoid possibly hurting your partner's feelings by not overruling. The tactful way to achieve the desired result is to tell your partner quietly that he has made a mistake and then let him overrule himself. If a call is changed from out to good, the point is replayed only if the out ball was put back in play.

15. *Audible or visible calls.* No matter how obvious it is to a player that his opponent's ball is out, the opponent is entitled to a prompt audible or visible out call.

16. *Opponent's calls questioned.* When a player genuinely doubts his opponent's call, the player may ask: "Are you sure of your call?" If the opponent reaffirms that the ball was out, his call shall be accepted. If the oppo-

nent acknowledges that he is uncertain, he loses the point. There shall be no further delay or discussion.

17. *Spectators never to make calls.* A player shall not enlist the aid of a spectator in making a call. No spectator has a part in the match.

18. *Prompt calls eliminate two chance option.* A player shall make all calls promptly after the ball has hit the court. A call shall be made either before the player's return shot has gone out of play or before the opponent has had the opportunity to play the return shot.

    Prompt calls will quickly eliminate the "two chances to win the point" option that some players practice. To illustrate, a player is advancing to the net for an easy put away when he sees a ball from an adjoining court rolling toward him. He continues his advance and hits the shot, only to have his supposed easy put away fly over the baseline. The player then claims a let. The claim is not valid because he forfeited his right to call a let by choosing instead to play the ball. He took his chance to win or lose, and he is not entitled to a second chance.

19. *Lets called when balls roll on the court.* When a ball from an adjacent court enters the playing area, any player shall call a let as soon as he becomes aware of the ball. The player loses the right to call a let if he unreasonably delays in making the call.

20. *Touches, hitting ball before it crosses net, invasion of opponent's court, double hits, and double bounces.* A player shall promptly acknowledge if:

    • a ball touches him;

    • he touches the net;

    • he touches his opponent's court;

    • he hits a ball before it crosses the net;

    • he deliberately carries or double hits the ball; or

    • the ball bounces more than once in his court.

21. *Balls hit through the net or into the ground.* A player shall make the ruling on a ball that his opponent hits through the net and on a ball that his opponent hits into the ground before it goes over the net.

22. *Calling balls on clay courts.* If any part of the ball mark touches the line on a clay court, the ball shall be called good. If you can see only part of the mark on the court, this means that the missing part is on the line or tape. A player should take a careful second look at any point-ending placement that is close to a line on a clay court. Occasionally a ball will strike the tape, jump, and then leave a full mark behind the line. The player should listen for the sound of the ball striking the tape and look for a clean spot on the tape near the mark. If these conditions exist, the player should give the point to his opponent.

SERVING

23. *Server's request for third ball.* When a server requests three balls, the receiver shall comply when the third ball is readily available. Distant balls shall be retrieved at the end of a game.

24. *Foot Faults.* A player may warn his opponent that the opponent has committed a flagrant foot fault. If the foot faulting continues, the player may attempt to locate an official. If no official is available, the player may call flagrant foot faults. Compliance with the foot fault rule is very much a function of a player's personal honor system. The plea that he should not be penalized because he only just touched the line and did not rush the net is not acceptable. Habitual foot faulting, whether intentional or careless, is just as surely cheating as is making a deliberate bad line call.

25. *Service calls in doubles.* In doubles the receiver's partner should call the service line, and the receiver should call the sideline and the center service line. Nonetheless, either partner may call a ball that he clearly sees.

26. *Service calls by serving team.* Neither the server nor his partner shall make a fault call on the first service even if they think it is out because the receiver may be giving the server the benefit of the doubt. But the server and his partner shall call out any second serve that either of them clearly sees out.

27. *Service let calls.* Any player may call a service let. The call shall be made before the return of serve goes out of play or is hit by the server or his partner. If the serve is an apparent or near ace, any let shall be called promptly.

28. *Obvious faults.* A player shall not put into play or hit over the net an obvious fault. To do so constitutes rudeness and may even be a form of gamesmanship. On the other hand, if a player believes that he cannot call a serve a fault and gives his opponent the benefit of a close call, the server is not entitled to replay the point.

29. *Receiver readiness.* The receiver shall play to the reasonable pace of the server. The receiver should make no effort to return a serve when he is not ready. If a player attempts to return a serve (even if it is a "quick" serve), then he (or his team) is presumed to be ready.

30. *Delays during service.* When the server's second service motion is interrupted by a ball coming onto the court, he is entitled to two serves. When there is a delay between the first and second serves:

    • the server gets one serve if he was the cause of the delay;

    • the server gets two serves if the delay was caused by the receiver or if there was outside interference.

The time it takes to clear a ball that comes onto the court between the first and second serves is not considered sufficient time to warrant the server receiving two serves unless this time is so prolonged as to constitute an interruption. The receiver is the judge of whether the delay is sufficiently prolonged to justify giving the server two serves.

SCORING

31. *Server announces score.* The server shall announce the game score before the first point of the game and the point score before each subsequent point of the game.

32. *Disputes.* Disputes over the score shall be resolved by using one of the following methods, which are listed in the order of preference:

    • count all points and games agreed upon by the players and replay only the disputed points or games;

    • play from a score mutually agreeable to all players;

    • spin a racket or toss a coin.

HINDRANCE ISSUES

33. *Talking during a point.* A player shall not talk while the ball is moving toward his opponent's side of the court. If the player's talking interferes with his oppo-

nent's ability to play the ball, the player loses the point. Consider the situation where a player hits a weak lob and loudly yells at his partner to get back. If the shout is loud enough to distract his opponent, then the opponent may claim the point based on a deliberate hindrance. If the opponent chooses to hit the lob and misses it, the opponent loses the point because he did not make a timely claim of hindrance.

34. *Feinting with the body.* A player may feint with his body while the ball is in play. He may change position at any time, including while the server is tossing the ball. Any movement or sound that is made solely to distract an opponent, including but not limited to waving the arms or racket or stamping the feet, is not allowed.

35. *Lets due to hindrance.* A let is not automatically grant-ed because of hindrance. A let is authorized only if the player could have made the shot had he not been hindered. A let is also not authorized for a hindrance caused by something within a player's control. For example, a request for a let because the player tripped over his own hat should be denied.

36. *Grunting.* A player should avoid grunting and mak-ing other loud noises. Grunting and other loud nois-es may bother not only opponents but also players on adjacent courts. In an extreme case, an opponent or a player on an adjacent court may seek the assistance of the referee or a roving official. The referee or official

may treat grunting and the making of loud noises as a hindrance. Depending upon the circumstance, this could result in a let or loss of point.

37. *Injury caused by a player.* When a player accidentally injures his opponent, the opponent suffers the consequences. Consider the situation where the server's racket accidentally strikes the receiver and incapacitates him. The receiver is unable to resume play within the time limit. Even though the server caused the injury, the server wins the match by retirement.

   On the other hand, when a player deliberately injures his opponent and affects the opponent's ability to play, then the opponent wins the match by default. Hitting a ball or throwing a racket in anger is considered a deliberate act.

WHEN TO CONTACT AN OFFICIAL

38. *Withdrawing from a match or tournament.* A player shall not enter a tournament and then withdraw when he discovers that tough opponents have also entered. A player may withdraw from a match or tournament only because of injury, illness, personal emergency, or another bona fide reason. If a player cannot play a match, he shall notify the referee at once so that his opponent may be saved a trip. A player who withdraws from a tournament is not entitled to the return of his entry fee unless he withdrew before the draw was made.

39. *Stalling.* The following actions constitute stalling:

    • warming up for more than the allotted time;

    • playing at about one-third a player's normal pace;

    • taking more than the allotted 90 seconds on the odd-game changeover;

    • taking a rest at the end of a set that contains an even number of games;

    • taking more than the authorized ten minutes during an authorized rest period between sets;

    • starting a discussion or argument in order for a player to catch his breath;

    • clearing a missed first service that doesn't need to be cleared; and

    • bouncing the ball ten times before each serve.

    Contact an official if you encounter a problem with stalling. It is subject to penalty under the Point Penalty System.

40. *Requesting an official.* While normally a player may not leave the playing area, he may visit the referee or seek a roving official to request assistance. Some reasons for visiting the referee include:

    • stalling;

    • chronic flagrant foot faults;

- a medical time-out

- a scoring dispute; and

- a pattern of bad calls.

A player may refuse to play until an official responds.

BALL ISSUES

41. *Retrieving stray balls.* Each player is responsible for removing stray balls and other objects from his end of the court. A player shall not go behind an adjacent court to retrieve a ball, nor shall he ask for return of a ball from players on an adjacent court until their point is over. When a player returns a ball that comes from an adjacent court, he shall wait until their point is over and then return it directly to one of the players, preferably the server.

42. *Catching a ball.* Unless you have made a local ground rule, if you catch a ball before it bounces, you lose the point regardless of where you are standing.

43. *New balls for a third set.* When a tournament specifies new balls for a third set, new balls shall be used unless all the players agree otherwise.

MISCELLANEOUS

44. *Clothing and equipment malfunction.* If clothing or equipment other than a racket becomes unusable

through circumstances outside the control of the player, play may be suspended for a reasonable period. The player may leave the court after the point is over to correct the problem. If a racket or string is broken, the player may leave the court to get a replacement, but he is subject to code violations under the Point Penalty System.

45. *Placement of towels.* Place towels on the ground outside the net post or at the back fence. Clothing and towels should never be placed on the net.

Appendixes

Appendix I—Regulations for Making Tests Specified in Rule 3

Appendix II—Procedures for Review and Hearings on the Rules of Tennis

Appendix III—The Wheelchair Tennis Player: Challenges and Procedures for a Player's Eligibility

Plan of the Court

Suggestions on How to Mark Out a Court

Amendment to the Rules

APPENDIX I
REGULATIONS FOR MAKING TESTS
SPECIFIED IN RULE 3

i. Unless otherwise specified all tests shall be made at a temperature of approximately 68° Fahrenheit (20° Centigrade) and a relative humidity of approximately 60 percent. All balls should be removed from their container and kept at the recognized temperature and humidity for 24 hours prior to testing, and shall be at that temperature and humidity when the test is commenced.

ii. Unless otherwise specified the limits are for a test conducted in an atmospheric pressure resulting in a barometric reading of approximately 30 inches (76cm.).

iii. Other standards may be fixed for localities where the average temperature, humidity or average barometric pressure at which the game is being played differ materially from 68° Fahrenheit (20° Centigrade), 60 percent and 30 inches (76cm.) respectively.

Applications for such adjusted standards may be made by any National Association to the International Tennis Federation and if approved shall be adopted for such localities.

iv. In all tests for diameter, a ring gauge shall be used consisting of a metal plate, preferably non-corrosive of a uniform thickness of one-eighth of an inch (.318 cm.). In the case of type 1 (fast) and type 2 (medium) balls, there shall be two circular openings in the plate measuring 2.575 inches (6.541 cm.) and 2.700 inches (6.858 cm.) in diameter, respectively. In the case of type 3 (slow) balls, there shall be two circular openings in the plate measuring 2.750 inches (6.985 cm.) and 2,875 inches (7.302 cm.) in diameter, respectively. The inner surface of the gauge shall have a convex profile with a radius of one-sixteenth of an inch (.159 cm.). The ball shall not drop through the smaller opening by its own weight and shall drop through the larger opening by its own weight.

v.   In all tests for deformation under Rule 3, the machine designed by Percy Herbert Stevens and patented in Great Britain under Patent No. 230250, together with the subsequent additions and improvements thereto, including the modifications required to take return deformations, shall be employed. Other machines may be specified to give equivalent readings to the Stevens machine and these may be used for testing ball deformation where such machines have been given approval by the International Tennis Federation.

vi.   Procedure for carrying out tests:

   a.   Pre-compression. Before any ball is tested it shall be steadily compressed by approximately one inch (2.54 cm.) on each of three diameters at right angles to one another in succession; this process to be carried out three times (nine compressions in all). All tests to be completed within two hours of pre-compression.

b. Bound test (as in Rule 3). Measurements are to be taken from the concrete base to the bottom of the ball.

c. Size test [as in paragraph (iv) above].

d. Weight test (as in Rule 3).

e. Deformation test. The ball is placed in position on the modified Stevens machine so that neither platen of the machine is in contact with the cover seam. The contact weight is applied, the pointer and the mark brought level, and the dials set to zero. The test weight equivalent to 18 lb. (8.165kg.) is placed on the beam and pressure applied by turning the wheel at a uniform speed so that five seconds elapse from the instant the beam leaves its seat until the pointer is brought level with the mark. When turning ceases the reading is recorded (forward deformation). The wheel is turned again until figure ten is reached on the scale [one inch (2.54 cm.) deformation]. The wheel is then rotated in the opposite direction at a uniform speed (thus releasing pressure) until the beam pointer again coincides with the mark. After waiting ten seconds the pointer is adjusted to the mark if necessary. The reading is then recorded (return deformation). This procedure is repeated on each ball across the two diameters at right angles to the initial position and to each other.

vii. *Classification of court surface pace.* The test method to be used for determining the pace of a court surface is test method ITF CS 01/01 (ITF surface pace rating) as described in the ITF publication entitled "An Initial ITF Study on Performance Standards for Tennis Court Surfaces."

Court surfaces which are found to have an ITF surface pace rating of between 0 and 35 shall be classified as being category 1 (slow pace). Examples of court surface types which conform to this classification will include most clay courts and other types of unbound mineral surfaces.

Court surfaces which are found to have an ITF surface pace rating of between 30 and 45 shall be classified as being category 2 (medium/medium-fast pace). Examples of court surface types which conform to this classification will include most hardcourts with various acrylic type coatings plus some textile surfaces.

Court surfaces which are found to have an ITF surface pace rating of over 40 shall be classified as being category 3 (fast pace). Examples of court surface types which conform to this classification will include most natural grass, artificial turf and some textile surfaces.

N.B. The proposed overlap in ITF surface pace rating values for the above categories is to allow some initial latitude in ball selection for the period of the experiment.

APPENDIX II
PROCEDURES FOR REVIEW AND HEARINGS ON THE RULES OF TENNIS

1. INTRODUCTION

1.1   These procedures were approved by the Board of Directors of the International Tennis Federation ("Board of Directors") on 17 May 1998.

1.2   The Board of Directors may from time to time supplement, amend, or vary these procedures.

2. OBJECTIVES

2.1   The International Tennis Federation is the custodian of the Rules of Tennis and is committed to:

a.   Preserving the traditional character and integrity of the game of tennis.

b.   Actively preserving the skills traditionally required to play the game.

c.   Encouraging improvements, which maintain the challenge of the game.

d.   Ensuring fair competition.

2.2   To ensure fair, consistent and expeditious review and hearings in relation to the Rules of Tennis the procedures set out below shall apply.

3. SCOPE

3.1   These Procedures shall apply to Rulings under:

   a.   Rule 1—The Court.

   b.   Rule 3—The Ball.

   c.   Rule 4—The Racket.

   d.   Appendix 1 of the Rules of Tennis.

   e.   Any other Rules of Tennis which the International Tennis Federation may decide.

4. STRUCTURE

4.1   Under these procedures Rulings shall be issued by a Ruling Board.

4.2   Such Rulings shall be final, save for an entitlement to appeal to an Appeal Tribunal pursuant to these procedures.

5. APPLICATION

5.1   Rulings shall be taken either:

a. Following a motion of the Board of Directors; or

b. Upon the receipt of an application in accordance with the procedures set out below.

6. APPOINTMENT AND COMPOSITION OF RULING BOARDS

6.1 Ruling Boards shall be appointed by the President of the International Tennis Federation ("President") or his designee and shall comprise of such number as the President or his designee shall determine.

6.2 If more than one person is appointed to the Ruling Board, the Ruling Board shall nominate one person from amongst themselves to act as Chairperson.

6.3 The Chairperson shall be entitled to regulate the procedures prior to and at any review and/or hearing of a Ruling Board.

7. PROPOSED RULINGS BY THE RULING BOARD

7.1 The details of any proposed Ruling issued upon the motion of the Board of Directors may be provided to any bona fide person or any players, equipment manufacturer or national association or members thereof with an interest in the proposed Ruling.

7.2   Any person so notified shall be given a reasonable period within which to forward comments, objections, or requests for information to the President or his designee in connection with the proposed Ruling.

8. APPLICATION FOR RULINGS

8.1   An application for a Ruling may be made by any party with a bona fide interest in the Ruling including any player, equipment manufacturer or national association or member thereof.

8.2   Any application for a Ruling must be submitted in writing to the President.

8.3   To be valid an application for a Ruling must include the following minimum information:

a.   The full name and address of the Applicant.

b.   The date of the application.

c.   A statement clearly identifying the interest of the Applicant in the question upon which a Ruling is requested.

d.   All relevant documentary evidence upon which the Applicant intends to rely at any hearing.

e.   If, in the opinion of the Applicant, expert evidence is necessary he shall include a request for such expert evidence to be heard. Such request must identify the name of any expert proposed and their relevant expertise.

f.   When an application for a Ruling on a racket or other piece of equipment is made, a prototype or exact copy of the equipment in question must be submitted with the application for a Ruling.

g.   If, in the opinion of the Applicant, there are extraordinary or unusual circumstances which require a Ruling to be made within a specified time or before a specified date he shall include a statement describing the extraordinary or unusual circumstances.

8.4   If an application for a Ruling does not contain the information and/or equipment referred to at Clause 8.3 (a)-(g) above the President or his designee shall notify the Applicant giving the Applicant a specified reasonable time within which to remedy the defect. If the Applicant fails to remedy the defect within the specified time the application shall be dismissed.

9. CONVENING THE RULING BOARD

9.1 On receipt of a valid application or on the motion of the Board of Directors the President or his designee may convene a Ruling Board to deal with the application or motion.

9.2 The Ruling Board need not hold a hearing to deal with an application or motion where the application or motion, in the opinion of the Chairperson, can be resolved in a fair manner without a hearing.

10. PROCEDURE OF THE RULING BOARD

10.1 The Chairperson of a Ruling Board shall determine the appropriate form, procedure and date of any review and/or hearing.

10.2 The Chairperson shall provide written notice of those matters set out at 10.1 above to any Applicant or any person or association who has expressed an interest in the proposed Ruling.

10.3 The Chairperson shall determine all matters relating to evidence and shall not be bound by judicial rules governing procedure and admissibility of evidence provided that the review and/or hearing is conducted in a fair manner with a reasonable opportunity for the relevant parties to present their case.

10.4 Under these procedures any review and/or hearings:

a. Shall take place in private.

b. May be adjourned and/or postponed by the Ruling Board.

10.5 The Chairperson shall have the discretion to co-opt from time to time additional members onto the Ruling Board with special skill or experience to deal with specific issues, which require such special skill or experience.

10.6 The Ruling Board shall take its decision by a simple majority. No member of the Ruling Board may abstain.

10.7 The Chairperson shall have the complete discretion to make such order against the Applicant (and/or other individuals or organisations commenting objecting or requesting information at any review and/or hearing) in relation to the costs of the application and/or the reasonable expenses incurred by the Ruling Board in holding tests or obtaining reports relating to equipment subject to a Ruling as he shall deem appropriate.

11. NOTIFICATION

11.1 Once a Ruling Board has reached a decision it shall provide written notice to the Applicant or any person or association who has expressed an interest in the proposed Ruling as soon as reasonably practicable.

11.2 Such written notice shall include a summary of the reasoning behind the decision of the Ruling Board.

11.3 Upon notification to the Applicant or upon such other date specified by the Ruling Board, the Ruling of the Ruling Board shall be immediately binding under the Rules of Tennis.

12. APPLICATION OF CURRENT RULES OF TENNIS

12.1 Subject to the power of the Ruling Board to issue interim Rulings, the current Rules of Tennis shall continue to apply until any review and/or hearing of the Ruling Board is concluded and a Ruling issued by the Ruling Board.

12.2 Prior to and during any review and/or hearing the Chairperson of the Ruling Board may issue such directions as are deemed reasonably necessary in the implementation of the Rules of Tennis and of these procedures including the issue of interim Rulings.

12.3 Such interim Rulings may include restraining orders on the use of any equipment under the Rules of Tennis pending a Ruling by the Ruling Board as to whether or not the equipment meets the specification of the Rules of Tennis.

13. APPOINTMENT AND COMPOSITION OF APPEAL TRIBUNALS

13.1 Appeal Tribunals shall be appointed by the President or his designee from [members of the Board of Directors/Technical Committee].

13.2 No member of the Ruling Board who made the original Ruling shall be a member of the Appeal Tribunal.

13.3 The Appeal Tribunal shall comprise of such number as the President or his designee shall determine but shall be no less than three.

13.4 The Appeal Tribunal shall nominate one person from amongst themselves to act as Chairperson.

13.5 The Chairperson shall be entitled to regulate the procedures prior to and at any appeal hearing.

14. APPLICATION TO APPEAL

14.1 An Applicant (or a person or association who has expressed an interest and forwarded any comments, objections, or requests to a proposed Ruling) may appeal any Ruling of the Ruling Board.

14.2 To be valid an application for an appeal must be:

a. Made in writing to the Chairperson of the Ruling Board who made the Ruling appealed not later than [45] days following notification of the Ruling;

b. Must set out details of the Ruling appealed against; and

c. Must contain the full grounds of the appeal.

14.3 Upon receipt of a valid application to appeal, the Chairperson of the Ruling Board making the original Ruling may require a reasonable appeal fee to be paid by the Appellant as a condition of appeal. Such appeal fee shall be repaid to the Appellant if the appeal is successful.

15. CONVENING THE APPEAL TRIBUNAL

15.1 The President or his designee shall convene the Appeal Tribunal following payment by the Appellant of any appeal fee.

16. PROCEDURES OF APPEAL TRIBUNAL

16.1 The Appeal Tribunal and their Chairperson shall conduct procedures and hearings in accordance with those matters set out in sections 10, 11 and 12 above.

16.2 Upon notification to the Appellant or upon such other date specified by the Appeal Tribunal the Ruling of the Appeal Tribunal shall be immediately binding and final under the Rules of Tennis.

17. GENERAL

17.1 If a Ruling Board consists of only one member that single member shall be responsible for regulating the hearing as Chairperson and shall determine the procedures to be followed prior to and during any review and/or hearing.

17.2 All reviews and/or hearings shall be conducted in English. In any hearing where an Applicant, and/or other individuals or organisations commenting, objecting or requesting information do not speak English an interpreter must be present. Wherever practicable the interpreter shall be independent.

17.3 The Ruling Board or Appeal Tribunal may publish extracts from its own Rulings.

17.4 All notifications to be made pursuant to these procedures shall be in writing.

17.5 Any notifications made pursuant to these procedures shall be deemed notified upon the date that they were communicated, sent or transmitted to the Applicant or other relevant party.

17.6 A Ruling Board shall have the discretion to dismiss an application if in its reasonable opinion the application is substantially similar to an application or motion upon which a Ruling Board has made a decision and/or Ruling within the 36 months prior to the date of the application.

APPENDIX III
THE WHEELCHAIR TENNIS PLAYER: CHALLENGES AND PROCEDURES FOR A PLAYER'S ELIGIBILITY

1. CHALLENGES

a.   The following parties have the right to question a player's eligibility:

- ITF Member Nations (through their General Secretary);

- The wheelchair tennis Players' Representatives Committee (through their Chairperson);

- The ITF Wheelchair Tennis Committee.

ITF Note: *ITA Member Nations who are not represented by their National Tennis Federation, may submit a challenge through the ITF Wheelchair Tennis Committee who must decide if the challenge should proceed to the Eligibility Sub-Committee.*

b.   On receipt of a formal written challenge from any of the parties named in 1. a. above, the ITF must inform the player and ask them to submit sufficient objective medical evidence of permanent physical disability in writing to the Eligibility Sub-Committee of the ITF Wheelchair

Tennis Committee within 28 days. The Eligibility Sub-Committee (which shall be made up of at least one medical doctor from the ITF Medical Commission and at least two ITF appointed experts in the Rules of Wheelchair Tennis) must then review the case.

ITF Note 1: The player may continue to play during the Eligibility Sub-Committee's investigation. Should the outcome of the Eligibility Sub-Committee be that the player does not meet the minimum criteria as laid out in Rule I of the Rules of Wheelchair Tennis, the player must then cease to play with immediate effect. The only exception to this is in the case of an appeal against the decision by the player as outlined in the Appeals Procedure below.

ITF Note 2: Failure to submit medical evidence as described above within 28 days of the request being made by the ITF shall result in automatic suspension of that player until such time as evidence is provided.

ITF Note 3: The costs incurred by the player in obtaining the medical evidence shall be borne by the player. All costs incurred in the evaluation of medical evidence provided by the player will be the responsibility of the ITF. The player will be instructed by the ITF, regarding how, when and where to provide the necessary medical evidence.

c. If the Eligibility Sub-Committee judges that a player is eligible to compete, their eligibility may not be challenged again for a minimum of 12 months. After this time, all challenges shall be subject to the same procedures as laid out above. If, after a second challenge, the player is still deemed eligible to compete, their eligibility may not be challenged again for a further 3 years.

ITF Note: *If a player is challenged after already having been deemed eligible to compete, they may continue to play while any new challenges are being considered.*

2. APPEALS PROCEDURE

a. If the Eligibility Sub-Committee judges that supporting medical evidence is insufficient, then the player may appeal within 14 days of the decision and request an evaluation by an independent medical doctor appointed by the ITF Member Nation for that player.

   Further to receiving the submission from the medical doctor appointed by the ITF Member Nation, the ITF Medical Commission will give a ruling on the eligibility of the player which shall not be subject to further appeal for a minimum of 12 months (see b. below).

ITF Note 1: *In the case of an appeal being made, the player may continue to play until after the appeal has been heard.*

ITF Note 2: *The costs of the evaluation for the appeal will be at the player's expense. All costs incurred in the evaluation of medical evidence provided by the medical doctor will be the responsibility of the ITF.*

b. If a person's circumstances change in relation to their physical disability in the future, the person is entitled to submit a request to the ITF to be reconsidered. This request may only be made a minimum of 12 months after the first appeal decision. Such a request shall be supported by the new medical evidence and shall be subject to the same process as outlined in Rule I of the Rules of Wheelchair Tennis and this Appendix III.

If, after the second appeal, the player is still deemed ineligible to compete, their case may not be reconsidered for a further 3 years.

ITF Note: *If the Eligibility Sub-Committee has already judged that a player is currently ineligible, they may not compete while any new medical evidence is being considered.*

PLAN OF THE COURT

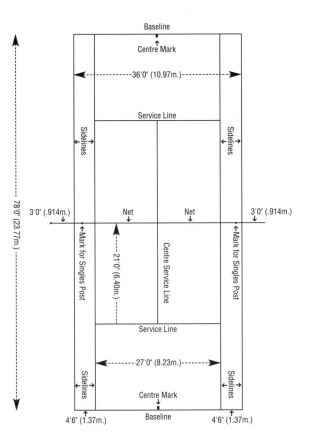

SUGGESTIONS ON HOW TO MARK OUT A COURT

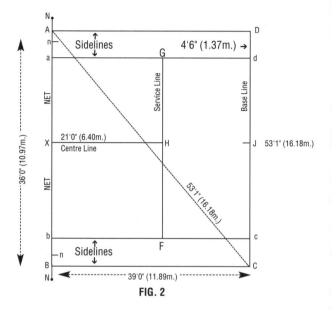

FIG. 2

The following procedure is for the usual combined Doubles and Singles Court. (See note at foot for a Court for one purpose only).

First select the position of the net; a straight line 42 feet (12.8m.) long. Mark the centre (X on the diagram above) and, measuring from there in each direction, mark:

- at 13'6" (4.11m.) the points a, b, where the net crosses the inner sidelines,

- at 16'6" (5.03m.) the positions of the singles posts (or sticks) (n, n),

- at 18'0" (5.49m.) the points A, B, where the net crosses the outer sidelines,

- at 21'0" (6.40m.) the positions of the net posts (N, N), being the ends of the original 42'0" (12.8m.) line.

Insert pegs at A and B and attach to them the respective ends of two measuring tapes. On one, which will measure the diagonal of the half-court, take a length 53'1" (16.18m.) and on the other (to measure the sideline) a length of 39'0" (11.89m.). Pull both taut so that at these distances they meet at a point C, which is one corner of the Court. Reverse the measurements to find the other corner D. As a check on this operation it is advisable at this stage to verify the length of the line CD which, being the base-line, should be found to be 36'0" (10.97m.); and at the same time its centre J can be marked, and also the ends of the inner sidelines (c, d), 4'6" (1.37m.) from C and D.

The centre-line and service-line are now marked by means of the points F, H, G, which are measured 21'0" (6.40m.) from the net down the lines bc, XJ, ad, respectively.

Identical procedure the other side of the net completes the Court.

ITF Note 1: If a Singles Court only is required, no lines are necessary outside the points a, b, c, d, but the Court can be measured out as above. Alternatively, the corners of the base-line (c, d) can be found if preferred by pegging the two tapes at a and b instead of at A and B, and by then using lengths of 47'5" (14.46m.) and 39'0" (11.89m.). The net posts will be at n, n, and a 33'0" (10m.) singles net should be used.

ITF Note 2: When a combined doubles and singles Court with a doubles net is used for singles, the net must be supported at the points n, n, to a height of 3 feet 6 inches (1.07m.) by means of two posts, called "singles sticks," which shall be not more than 3 inches (7.5cm.) square or 3 inches (7.5cm.) in diameter. The centres of the singles sticks shall be 3 feet (.914m.) outside the singles Court on each side.

To assist in the placing of these singles sticks it is desirable that the points n, n, should each be shown with a white dot when the Court is marked.

USTA Comment on Tennis Court Layout

All Courts should be laid out for singles and doubles play. The same lines—except for the sideline extensions for doubles play—are required for each.

Courts in the northern two-thirds of the United States should generally be laid out with the long axis north and south; it is advantageous, however, to orient the Courts in the southern one-third of the country 15°-25° west of true (not magnetic) north in order to minimize the adverse effects of the afternoon winter sun.

Figure 1 indicates the exact dimensions of the lines as well as recommended side and back spacing. Note that the dimensions shown in the diagram are measurements to the outside edge of the lines. For regulation play, the space behind the baseline (between the baseline and fence) should not be less than 21 feet, for an overall dimension of 60' x 120'. For stadium Courts, this perimeter spacing should be increased to allow space for line umpires without impeding the players. (See Rule 1.) Net posts should be located with their centers three feet outside the doubles sideline.

Most Courts are laid out with lines two inches (5cm.) wide. Lines may be one inch (2.5cm.) to two inches (5cm.) wide excepting the center service line which must be two inches (5cm.) wide and the baselines which may be up to four inches (10cm.) wide.

For more detailed information on the subject, *Tennis Courts,* a book containing United States Tennis Association and U.S. Tennis Court and Track Builders Association recommendations for the construction, maintenance, and equipment needs of a tennis Court installation, can be obtained by contacting the USTA Bookstore, 70 West Red Oak Lane, White Plains, NY 10604-3602.

AMENDMENTS TO THE RULES
INTERNATIONAL TENNIS FEDERATION RULE 69

USTA Comment
The ITF, not the USTA, is responsible for the Rules of
Tennis. Amendments to the Rules of Tennis are made
through the procedures of the ITF. Rule 69 of the ITF
controls the manner in which amendments may be made
to the Rules of Tennis.

The official and decisive text to the Rules of Tennis shall be
forever in the English language and no alteration or interpretation of such Rules shall be made except at an Annual
General Meeting of the Council, nor unless notice of the
resolution embodying such alteration shall have been re-
ceived by the Federation in accordance with Article 16 of
the Constitution of ITF Ltd. (Notice of Resolutions) and
such resolution or one having the like effect shall be carried
by a majority of two-thirds of the votes recorded in respect
of the same.

Any alteration so made shall take effect as from the
first day of January following unless the Meeting shall by
the like majority decide otherwise.

The Board of Directors shall have power, however, to
settle all urgent questions of interpretation subject to con-
firmation at the General Meeting next following.

This Rule shall not be altered at any time without the
unanimous consent of a General Meeting of the Council.